WORLD PREM

CW00329265

ABBEY THEATRE
THE HANGING GARDENS
A NEW PLAY BY
FRANK MCGUINNESS

Premiered by the Abbey Theatre
on the Abbey stage on 9 October 2013.

The Abbey Theatre gratefully acknowledges
the financial support of the Arts Council of
Ireland and the support of the Department
of the Arts, Heritage and the Gaeltacht.

ABBEY
THEATRE
AMHARCLANN
NA MAINISTREACH

THE ABBEY THEATRE is Ireland's national theatre. It was founded by W.B. Yeats and Lady Augusta Gregory. Since it first opened its doors in 1904 the theatre has played a vital and often controversial role in the literary, social and cultural life of Ireland.

We place the writer and theatre-maker at the heart of all that we do, commissioning and producing exciting new work and creating discourse and debate on the political, cultural and social issues of the day. Our aim is to present great theatre art in a national context so that the stories told on stage have a resonance with artists and audiences alike.

In 1905 the Abbey Theatre first toured internationally and continues to be an ambassador for Irish arts and culture worldwide.

Over the years, the Abbey Theatre has nurtured and premiered the work of major playwrights such as J.M. Synge and Sean O'Casey as well as contemporary classics from Sebastian Barry, Marina Carr, Bernard Farrell, Brian Friel, Thomas Kilroy, Frank McGuinness, Tom MacIntyre, Tom Murphy, Mark O'Rowe and Billy Roche.

We support a new generation of Irish writers at the Abbey Theatre including Richard Dormer, Gary Duggan, Stacey Gregg, Nancy Harris, Elaine Murphy and Carmel Winters.

None of this can happen without our audiences and our supporters. Annie Horniman provided crucial financial support to the Abbey in its first years. Many others have followed her lead by investing in and supporting our work.

We also acknowledge the financial support of the Arts Council for our programme.

IS Í AMHARCLANN NA MAINISTREACH amharclann náisiúnta na hÉireann. W.B. Yeats agus an Bantiarna Augusta Gregory a bhunaigh í. Riamh anall ón uair a osclaíodh a doirse i 1904, ghlac an amharclann ról an-tábhachtach agus, go minic, ról a bhí sách conspóideach, i saol liteartha, sóisialta agus cultúrtha na hÉireann.

Tá an scríobhneoir agus and t-amharclannóir i gcroílár a dhéanaimid anseo san amharclann, trí shaothar nua spreagúil a choimisiúnú agus a léiriú agus trí dhioscúrsa agus díospóireacht a chruthú i dtaobh cheisteanna polaitiúla, cultúrtha agus sóisialta na linne. Is í an aidhm atá againn ealaín amharclannaíochta den scoth a láithriú i gcomhthéacs náisiúnta ionas go mbeidh dáimh ag lucht ealaíne agus lucht féachana araon leis na scéalta a bhíonn á n-aithris ar an stáitse.

I 1905 is ea a chuaigh complacht Amharclann na Mainistreach ar camchuairt idirnáisiúnta den chéad uair agus leanann sí i gcónaí de bheith ina hambasadóir ar fud an domhain d'ealaíona agus cultúr na hÉireann.

In imeacht na mblianta, rinne Amharclann na Mainistreach saothar mórdhrámadóirí ar nós J.M. Synge agus Sean O'Casey a chothú agus a chéadléiriú, mar a rinne sí freisin i gcás clasaicí comhaimseartha ó dhrámadóirí amhail Sebastian Barry, Marina Carr, Bernard Farrell, Brian Friel, Thomas Kilroy, Frank McGuinness, Tom MacIntyre, Tom Murphy, Mark O'Rowe agus Billy Roche.

Tugaimid tacaíocht chomh maith don ghlúin nua Scríbhneoirí Éireannacha in Amharclann na Mainistreach, lena n-áirítear Richard Dormer, Gary Duggan, Stacey Gregg, Nancy Harris, Elaine Murphy agus Carmel Winters.

Ní féidir aon ní den chineál sin a thabhairt i gcrích gan ár lucht féachana agus ár lucht tacaíochta. Sholáthair Annie Horniman tacaíocht airgid ríthábhachtach don Mhainistir siar i mblianta tosaigh na hamharclainne. Lean iliomad daoine eile an dea-shampla ceannródaíochta sin uaithi ó shin trí infheistíocht a dhéanamh inár gcuid oibre agus tacaíocht a thabhairt dúinn.

Táimid fíor bhuíoch don tacaíocht airgeadais atá le fail ón Chomhairle Ealaíon.

CAST (IN ALPHABETICAL ORDER)	
Rachel Grant	Cathy Belton
Jane Grant	Barbara Brennan
Sam Grant	Niall Buggy
Charlie Grant	Declan Conlon
Maurice Grant	Marty Rea

Director	Patrick Mason
Set Design	Michael Pavelka
Lighting Design	Davy Cunningham
Costume Design	Joan O'Clery
Sound Design	Denis Clohessy
Voice Director	Andrea Ainsworth
Stage Manger	Brendan Galvin
Deputy Stage Manger	Anne Kyle
Assistant Stage Manger	Orla Burke
Casting Director	Kelly Phelan
Hair and Make-Up	Val Sherlock
Photography	Ros Kavanagh
Graphic Design	Zero-G
Set Construction	Capital Scenery Ltd.
Sign Language Interpreter	Caroline O'Leary
Audio Description	Bríd Ní Ghruagáin
	Maureen Portsmouth
Captioning	Ruth McCreery

THANKS TO

Nicole Edey, Charley Fone, Olivia Jonker, Michael Leopold, Emma Robinson,
Cécile Trémolières, Katie Unsworth-Murray, Amy Watts and Amy Whittle for
providing design assistance to Michael Pavelka.

*Audio described and captioned performances are provided by Arts and Disability
Ireland with funding from the Arts Council / An Chomhairle Ealaíon.*

WORLD PREMIERE

ABBEY THEATRE
THE HANGING GARDENS

A NEW PLAY BY

FRANK MCGUINNESS

SPECIAL THANKS TO

M•A•C Cosmetics for providing make-up products for this production.

Please note that the text of the play which appears in this volume may be changed during the rehearsal process and appear in a slightly altered form in performance.

Biogra-
phies

FRANK MCGUINNESS

WRITER

FRANK'S WORK AT the Abbey Theatre includes his dramatization of James Joyce's *The Dead*, an adaptation of Ibsen's *John Gabriel Borkman, Dolly West's Kitchen* (and Old Vic, London, nominated for an Olivier Award 2001), *The Bird Sanctuary, Lorca's Yerma, The Factory Girls, Carthaginians* (also Hampstead Theatre, London), *Baglady* and *Observe the Sons of Ulster Marching towards the Somme*, which won the London Evening Standard Most Promising Playwright Award, the Rooney Prize for Irish Literature, Harvey's Best Play Award, the Cheltenham Literary Prize, the Plays and Players Award, the Ewart - Briggs Peace Prize and the London Fringe Award. Other theatre work includes *Innocence* and *The Bread Man* (Gate Theatre), *Gates of Gold* (Gate Theatre and Finborough Theatre, London), *Someone Who'll Watch Over Me* (Hampstead Theatre, West End and Broadway), Winner of the New York Critics Circle Award and the Writers Guild Award for Best Play, *Mutabilitie* (National Theatre, London), *Speaking Like Magpies* and *Mary and Lizzie* (Royal Shakespeare Company), *There Came a Gypsy Riding* (Almeida Theatre, London), *Greta Garbo Came to Donegal* (Tricycle Theatre, London), *The Match Box* (Tricycle Theatre, London and Liverpool Playhouse) and *Crocodile* (Sky Arts Live and Riverside Studios). Frank's widely performed adaptations of classic plays include Ibsen's *Rosmersholm*, Brecht's *The Caucasian Chalk Circle*, De Molina's *Damned by Despair* and Sophocles' *Oedipus* (National Theatre, London), Brecht's *The Threepenny Opera* (Gate Theatre), *Peer Gynt* (Gate Theatre, Royal Shakespeare Company, International Tour and National Theatre, London), Chekhov's *Three Sisters* (Gate Theatre and Royal Court), *Hedda Gabler* (Roundabout, Broadway), *Uncle Vanya* (Field Day Production), *A Doll's House* (Playhouse Theatre, Broadway), Winner of the Tony Award for Best Revival and the Outer Critics Circle Award, Racine's *Phaedra* (Donmar Warehouse), *Sophocles' Electra* (Chichester, Donmar Warehouse and Barrymore Theatre, Broadway), Ostrovsky's *The Storm* (Almeida Theatre, London), Strindberg's *Miss Julie* (Theatre Royal Haymarket, London), Euripedes' *Hecuba* (Donmar Warehouse), a dramatization of Du Maurier's *Rebecca* (David Pugh productions and UK Tour), Ibsen's *Ghosts* (Bristol Old Vic and Duchess Theatre, London), *The Lady from the Sea* (Arcola Theatre) and Euripides' *Helen* (Shakespeare's Globe). Film and television work includes *Scout, The Hen House, Dancing at Lughnasa, The Stranger* (BAFTA Nomination) and *A Short Stay in Switzerland* (Broadcast Prize and BAFTA Nomination). Frank is currently working on an opera cycle based on the *Oedipus Trilogy* with the composer Julian Anderson for the ENO. Frank lectures in English at University College Dublin. He was born in Buncrana, Co. Donegal and now lives in Dublin.

PATRICK MASON
DIRECTOR

PATRICK IS A freelance director of theatre and opera. He has had a long association with the Abbey Theatre, which culminated in his tenure as Artistic Director from 1993 - 1999. He has worked extensively with writers such as Brian Friel, Hugh Leonard, Tom Murphy, Tom Kilroy and Tom MacIntyre. His production of Friel's *Dancing at Lughnasa* won him an Olivier nomination in 1991 and a Tony Award for Best Director in 1992. He is also closely associated with the work of Frank McGuinness and at the Abbey Theatre directed the premieres of *The Factory Girls, Observe the Sons of Ulster Marching Towards the Somme* and *Dolly West's Kitchen* (also Old Vic, London) and at the Gate Theatre he directed *Gates of Gold*. Recent work at the Gate Theatre includes *The Yalta Game* (Sydney/Edinburgh Festivals), *Hay Fever* (Charleston Spoleto Festival) and *The Speckled People*. Opera work includes productions for Wexford Festival Opera, WNO and ENO, as well as productions for Opera Zuid, Opera Ireland and Buxton Festival. In 2000 he was awarded an honorary doctorate by Trinity College Dublin in recognition of his contribution to Irish Theatre. Patrick is currently an adjunct professor in Drama at University College Dublin and was conferred with an honorary doctorate by the university in 2013.

MICHAEL PAVELKA
SET DESIGN

THIS IS MICHAEL'S debut at the Abbey Theatre. As a stage designer he has worked on over 170 shows. He is a founder member of Propeller Theatre and has designed all of their world-touring ensemble Shakespeare productions including *Rose Rage* (Chicago Shakespeare Theater, transferring to New York) for which he was nominated Best Costume Design at Chicago's Jeff Awards 2004 and *The Merchant of Venice*, Winner of the TMA's Best Set Design 2009. Other theatre work includes *Death of a Salesman* and *Hay Fever* (Gate Theatre), *The Fishing Trip* and *Holiday* directed by Lindsay Anderson (Old Vic Theatre, London). In London's West End; *A Few Good Men, Absurd Person Singular, The Constant Wife, How the Other Half Loves, Other People's Money, Leonardo, Blues in the Night* (also Dublin, New York and Tokyo), *Macbeth, A Midsummer Night's Dream, Rose Rage, Twelfth Night* and *The Taming of the Shrew* (Old Vic Theatre, London). Other classical works include *The Life of Galileo*, Winner Best Design Manchester Evening News Theatre Awards 1996, *The Resistible Rise of Arturo Ui, The Caucasian Chalk Circle, Measure for Measure, A Midsummer Night's Dream*, Winner Best Production Manchester Evening News Awards 1992, *The Good Soul of Szechuan, Oliver*

Twist and *Great Expectations* (Library Theatre, Manchester), *Twelfth Night* (Seattle Repertory Theatre), *The Odyssey*, *The Two Gentlemen of Verona, Henry V* and *Julius Caesar* (Royal Shakespeare Company, Stratford and the Barbican Theatre) and *Edmond* (National Theatre, London). Michael designed the first African language production of *Mother Courage and Her Children* in Kampala at the National Theatre of Uganda, Kennedy Center, Washington DC and Grahamstown Festival, RSA. Dance designs include *Revelations* (Queen Elizabeth Hall, London's South Bank) and *Off the Wall*, which opened the refurbished Royal Festival Hall in 2007. Michael trained at Wimbledon College of Art, London. His work represented the UK at the Prague Quadrennial for world stage design in 2011.

DAVY CUNNINGHAM
LIGHTING DESIGN

DAVY'S PREVIOUS WORK at the Abbey Theatre includes *The House of Bernarda Alba* and *Big Maggie*. He has worked extensively in both theatre and opera and has lit over 150 opera productions worldwide. Theatre work includes *An Enemy of the People* and *Mrs Warren's Profession* (Gate Theatre), *The Playboy of the Western World* (also touring Ireland and New York), *The Well of the Saints, The Tinker's Wedding* and *The Silver Tassie* (Druid), *Ivanov, Much Ado about Nothing* and

Nicol Williamson's one man show *Jack* (West End, London), *The Taming of The Shrew* (Royal Shakespeare Company), *The Miser* (National Theatre, London), five productions at the Old Vic, *Othello* and five Christmas productions (Royal Lyceum, Edinburgh), *The Missing* (National Theatre of Scotland), *Julius Caesar* (Birmingham Rep) and *Hamlet* (Rapture, Scottish tour 2005).

JOAN O'CLERY
COSTUME DESIGN

JOAN'S PREVIOUS WORK at the Abbey Theatre includes *Major Barbara, Translations, The Plough and the Stars* (2010), *Christ Deliver Us!, The Last Days of a Reluctant Tyrant, The Importance of Being Earnest, Hamlet, A Doll's House, The Wild Duck, Lolita,* Winner Best Costume Design Irish Times Theatre Awards 2002, *A Whistle in the Dark* and *The Colleen Bawn*. Other theatre work includes *A Streetcar Named Desire, An Enemy of the People, Arcadia, Boston Marriage, Endgame, Watt, Celebration, God of Carnage, Oleanna, Molly Sweeney* and *The Pinter Festival,* Winner Best Costume Design Irish Times Theatre Awards 1997 (Gate Theatre), *Peer Gynt,* Winner Best Costume Design Irish Times Theatre Awards 2012 (Rough Magic Theatre Company), *The Girl Who Forgot To Sing Badly* (The Ark/Theatre Lovett), *DruidMurphy* (Druid), *The Crucible* (Lyric Theatre,

Belfast), *The Taming of the Shrew* and *Macbeth* (Royal Shakespeare Company, Stratford and West End). Dance and opera work includes The *Rite of Spring* and *Swept* (CoisCéim Dance Theatre), *Scheherezade* (Ballet Ireland), *Turandot* and *Dead Man Walking* (Opera Ireland), *Aida* (Lyric Opera), *La Traviata* (English National Opera at the London Coliseum) and *Moses* (Theatre St Gallen). Film work includes *Snap*, *Swansong* and *The Story of Occi Byrne* and *King of The Travellers* (both IFTA nominated for Best Costume Design).

DENIS CLOHESSY

ORIGINAL MUSIC & SOUND DESIGN

DENIS' WORK AT the Abbey Theatre includes *Shush, Shibari, The Government Inspector, Perve, The Rivals, The Resistible Rise of Arturo Ui, An Ideal Husband, Three Sisters, The Seafarer, Romeo and Juliet, The Crucible, Julius Caesar, Big Love, Burial at Thebes, Fool for Love* and *Woman and Scarecrow*. Other theatre work includes *Mrs. Warren's Profession, A Woman of No Importance, My Cousin Rachel, Da, Hay Fever, Watt, Molly Sweeney, Cat on a Hot Tin Roof, BPM Festival - Beckett Pinter Mamet, Death of a Salesman, Arcadia, Present Laughter, All My Sons, Faith Healer, Afterplay, The Yalta Game, The Real Thing, Festen* and *Hedda Gabler* (Gate Theatre), *Sodome, My Love,* Winner Best Sound Irish Times Theatre Awards 2010, *The Importance of Being Earnest, Life is a Dream, Attempts on Her Life, Don Carlos* and *Dream of Autumn,* (Rough Magic Theatre Company), *Man of Valour,* Winner Best Design ABSOLUT Fringe Award 2011 and *Happy Days* (Corn Exchange), *Silent* and *The Pride of Parnell Street* (Fishamble: The New Play Company), *Zoe's Play* (The Ark), *Macbeth* (Lyric Theatre, Belfast), *Dusk Ahead* and *The Falling Song* (Junk Ensemble) and *The Shawshank Redemption* (Lane Productions). Film work includes *His and Hers, Undressing My Mother, Useless Dog,* for which he won Best Soundtrack at the 2005 European Short Film Biennale in Stuttgart (Venom Films), *The Limits of Liberty* (South Wind Blows), *The Irish Pub* (Atom Films), *In Sunshine or in Shadow* and *A Bloody Canvas* (Fastnet Films), *The Reluctant Revolutionary* and *Her Mother's Daughters* (Underground Films).

CATHY BELTON

RACHEL GRANT

CATHY'S PREVIOUS WORK at the Abbey Theatre includes *The House, 16 Possible Glimpses, John Gabriel Borkman* (also toured to BAM, New York), *The Plough and the Stars* (2010), *Christ Deliver Us!, Only an Apple, The Recruiting Officer, The Crucible, The School for Scandal, The Playboy of the Western World* (tour of Ireland and the US), *The Burial at Thebes, The Plough and the Stars* (2003), *A Whistle in the Dark, Tartuffe, Medea, The Broken Jug, Living Quarters, A Crucial Week in the Life of a Grocer's Assistant* and *Silverlands*. Other theatre work includes *The Housekeeper*, Irish Times Theatre Award nomination for Best Actress 2012, *Solemn Mass for a Full Moon in Summer* and *Shiver* (Rough Magic Theatre Company), *Anything But Love* (Belltable Arts Centre), *The Making of 'Tis Pity She's A Whore* (Siren Productions), *Strandline* (Fishamble: The New Play Company), *The Playboy of the Western World* (Druid, Tokyo Arts Festival), *Uncle Vanya, Festen, A View from the Bridge, Betrayal, A Woman of No Importance* and *The Last Summer* (Gate Theatre), *Skylight* (Landmark Productions), *Silas Marner* and *Women in Arms,* Irish Times/ESB Award nomination for Best Actress 2002 (Storytellers Theatre Company), *Tiné Cnámh, An Triail, Scothsceálta* (Amharclann de hÍde), *True Lines* (Bickerstaffe Theatre Company), *Buddleia* and *Kitchensink* (The Passion Machine), *The Tempest, Romeo and Juliet* and *Hamlet* (Island Theatre Company) and *Eclipsed* (Town Hall Theatre, Galway). Television and film credits include *The Clinic, Glenroe, Paths to Freedom* and *Proof* (RTÉ), *Single Handed* (RTÉ and ITV), *Doctors* (BBC), *Roy*, IFTA nomination for Best Supporting Actress 2013 (BBC and

Jam Media), *The Other Side of Sleep* (Fastnet Films), *Little Foxes* (Samson Films), *Savage* (SP Films), *The Tiger's Tail* (Merlin Films), *Intermission* (IFC Films), *Before I Sleep* (Brother Films), *Tupperware* (Buena Vista International), *Philomena* (BBC Films and Baby Cow Productions) and *A Little Chaos* (BBC Films and Lionsgate UK). Radio for BBC and RTÉ includes *The Silver Fox, The Power of Darkness, Departures, The Plough and the Stars, The Beebox, Performances, Juno and the Paycock, The Irish RM, Anything But Love* and *Talk To Me Like The Rain.* Cathy graduated from Trinity College, Dublin with a degree in Drama and English.

BARBARA BRENNAN
JANE GRANT

BARBARA'S PREVIOUS WORK at the Abbey Theatre includes *Shush, Big Love, Woman and Scarecrow, Lovers at Versailles, Down the Line, A Life, The Colleen Bawn, Kevin's Bed, A Picture of Paradise, The Importance of Being Earnest, A Woman of No Importance, She Stoops to Folly, Six Characters in Search of an Author, The Hostage, Angels in America, The Lilly Lally Show, Chamber Music, The Iceman Cometh, Drama at Inish, One Last White Horse* and *The Glass Menagerie.* Other theatre work includes *The Heiress*, Winner Irish Theatre Award for Best Actress 1979, *A Streetcar*

Named Desire, Winner Irish Theatre Award for Best Supporting Actress 1981, *Hedda Gabbler,* Irish Theatre Award nomination for Best Actress 1984, *Salomé, A Christmas Carol, Pygmalion, The Eccentricities of a Nightingale, Pride and Prejudice, The Beckett Festival, Festen, The Deep Blue Sea, Jane Eyre, Hayfever, Present Laughter* and *All My Sons* (Gate Theatre), *Cabaret* (Olympia Theatre), *By the Bog of Cats* (Wyndams Theatre, London), *Honour* (b*spoke theatre company), *Sleeping Beauty* and *Alice in Wonderland* (Landmark Productions), *Macbeth* and *The Making of 'Tis Pity She's a Whore* (Siren Productions) and *Steel Magnolias* (Gaiety Theatre and National Tour). Film and television work includes *The Clinic, No Tears* and *Hell for Leather* (RTÉ), *Veronica Guerin* (Merrion Film Productions) and *The Tudors* (Showtime Productions).

NIALL BUGGY
SAM GRANT

NIALL HAS HAD a long association with the Abbey Theatre with a career spanning over four decades. His previous work at the Abbey Theatre includes *Drama at Inish, The Cherry Orchard, The Hostage, A State of Chassis, The Rising of the Moon, The Seagull* and *Hadrian VII.* He has worked extensively on the stage and screen in Ireland, the UK and the

US. Theatre work includes the 2012 nationwide tour of *DruidMurphy* (Druid), *Uncle Vanya,* Winner Best Actor in the Irish Times Theatre Awards 1998 (Gate Theatre), *Dead Funny,* Winner Olivier Award for Best Comedy Performance 1995 (Vaudeville Theatre, London), *Juno and the Paycock,* Winner Best Actor in the T.M.A Awards 1993 (Wyndham's Theatre, London) and *Aristocrats,* Winner of the Time Out Award, Obie Award in New York, Drama Desk Award and a Clarence Derwent Award 1989 (Hampstead Theatre, London). Film work includes *Jack Taylor 3* (Taylor Made Films Ltd), *The Duel, Mamma Mia, Casanova, The Butcher Boy, Alien 3, The Playboys* and *Turner.* Television work includes *Inspector Lewis, Dalziel and Pascoe, Father Ted, The Bill* and *The Professionals.*

DECLAN CONLON
CHARLIE GRANT

DECLAN'S PREVIOUS WORK at the Abbey Theatre includes *Drum Belly, Quietly,* (toured to Traverse Theatre, Edinburgh as part of the Edinburgh Festival Fringe), Winner The Scotsman Fringe First Award 2013, *The House,* Winner Irish Times Theatre Award for Best Actor 2012, *Terminus* (National and International tour), Manchester Theatre Awards nomination for Best Actor 2011, *The Last Days of a Reluctant Tyrant, A Whistle in the*

Dark, Famine, The Patriot Game, The Burial at Thebes, The Crucible, The Recruiting Officer, Julius Caesar, A Month in The Country, Winner Irish Times Theatre Award for Best Supporting Actor 2006, *True West, The Hamlet Project, All My Sons, Henry IV* (Part 1), *Heavenly Bodies, What Happened Bridgie Cleary,* and *The Last Ones.* Other theatre work includes *An Enemy of the People, The Last Summer, The Book of Evidence* (originally produced in conjunction with Kilkenny Arts Festival) and *The Importance of Being Earnest* (Gate Theatre), *Juno and the Paycock* (Gaiety Theatre), *The Sanctuary Lamp* (b*spoke theatre company), *Improbable Frequency* and *Copenhagen,* Irish Times Theatre Award nomination for Best Actor 2002 (Rough Magic Theatre Company), *Freefall* and *Cat on a Hot Tin Roof* (Corn Exchange), *Miss Julie* and *The Country* (Project Arts Centre), *As You Like It, The Spanish Tragedy, La Lupa, The Mysteries* and *Henry VI* (Royal Shakespeare Company), *The Walls, The Ends of the Earth* and *The Machine Wreckers* (National Theatre, London), *Macbeth* (West End), *Our Country's Good* (Young Vic) and *Uncle Vanya* (Lyric Theatre, Belfast). Television work includes *The Tudors* (Showtime), *Fair City, Amber, Raw, Trouble in Paradise, Proof* and *Bachelors Walk* (RTÉ), *Single Handed* (RTÉ and ITV), *Anytime Now, Dangerfield* and *The Family* (BBC) and

Cromwell (Title Films). Film credits include *Love Eternal, Calvary, Basket Case, Debris, Hereafter, The Trouble with Sex, Honest, All Souls Day* and *Roman Spring of Mrs Stone.* Radio work includes *The Burial at Thebes* and *The Hounds of the Baskerville.*

MARTY REA
MAURICE GRANT

MARTY'S PREVIOUS WORK at the Abbey Theatre includes *Major Barbara, John Gabriel Borkman* (also toured to BAM, New York), *The Rivals, Only an Apple, An Ideal Husband, The Big House, Saved* and *The Importance of Being Earnest.* Other theatre work includes *Conversations on a Homecoming, Whistle in the Dark* and *Famine* (DruidMurphy), *My Cousin Rachel, Little Women, Hay Fever, Arcadia, The Glass Menagerie* and *Salomé* (Gate Theatre), *Hamlet,* Winner Irish Times Theatre Awards for Best Actor 2010 and *Philadelphia, Here I Come!* (Second Age Theatre Company), *Improbable Frequency* (New York tour), *Pentecost* and *Spokesong* (Rough Magic Theatre Company) and *Observe the Sons of Ulster Marching Towards the Somme* (Livin' Dred Theatre Company). Marty graduated from Royal Academy of Dramatic Art, London in 2002.

The Abbey Theatre would like to thank the supporters of the <u>110th Anniversary</u> <u>Campaign</u> 1904–2014

'We have established the Abbey Theatre's 110th Anniversary Fund to ensure we continue to fuel the flame our founders lit over a century ago. I am proud to be a supporter of the 110th Campaign by being a Guardian of the Abbey Theatre. With your support we can develop playwrights, support Ireland's theatre artists, engage Irish citizens and present world renowned theatre both nationally and internationally.'

Fiach Mac Conghail, Director / Stiúrthóir

CORPORATE GUARDIANS

The Westbury Hotel
DUBLIN

The Doyle Collection, official hotel partner of Ireland's national theatre.

  BROWN THOMAS

Do more.

McCANN FITZGERALD Irish Life

 Bank of Ireland   ARTHUR COX

MEDIA PARTNERS

Sunday Independent

Irish Independent

SUPPORTER OF THE NEW PLAYWRIGHTS PROGRAMME

Deloitte.

CORPORATE AMBASSADORS

Paddy Power
101 Talbot Restaurant
Bewley's
Wynn's Hotel
Abbey Travel
CRH
Conway Communications
The Merrion Hotel
Baker Tilly Ryan Glennon
National Radio Cabs
The Church Café Bar
Clarion Consulting
Limited
Westin Hotels & Resorts
Manor House Hotels
of Ireland
Zero-G
Irish Poster Advertising
Bad Ass Café Temple Bar

CORPORATE AMBASSADORS

Spector Information
Security
ely bar & brasserie
University College Cork

CORPORATE PARTNERS

AIB
High Performance
Management

SUPPORTING CAST

Anraí Ó Braonáin
Joe Byrne
Kevin Walsh
Susan McGrath
Oonagh Desire
Róise Goan
John Daly
Zita Byrne

GUARDIANS OF THE ABBEY

Mrs. Carmel Naughton
Sen. Fiach Mac Conghail

FELLOWS OF THE ABBEY

Frances Britton
Catherine Byrne
Sue Cielinski
Dónall Curtin
Tommy Gibbons
James Hickey
Dr. John Keane
Andrew Mackey
Eugene Magee
James McNally
Gerard & Liv McNaughton
Donal Moore
Pat Moylan
Elizabeth Purcell Cribbin
Marie Rogan & Paul Moore
Mark Ryan

Abbey Theatre
Staff & Supporters

The Abbey Theatre gratefully acknowledges the financial support of the Arts Council of Ireland and the support of the Department of the Arts, Heritage and the Gaeltacht.

Archive partner of the Abbey Theatre.

The Hanging Gardens

Frank McGuinness was born in Buncrana, Co. Donegal, and now lives in Dublin and lectures in English at University College Dublin. His plays include *The Factory Girls* (1982), *Baglady* (1985), *Observe the Sons of Ulster Marching Towards the Somme* (1985), *Innocence* (1986), *Carthaginians* (1988), *Mary and Lizzie* (1989), *The Bread Man* (1991), *Someone Who'll Watch Over Me* (1992), *The Bird Sanctuary* (1994), *Mutabilitie* (1997), *Dolly West's Kitchen* (1999), *Gates of Gold* (2002), *Speaking Like Magpies* (2005), *There Came a Gypsy Riding* (2007), *Greta Garbo Came to Donegal* (2010) and *The Match Box* (2012). Among his many widely staged versions are *Rosmersholm* (1987), *Peer Gynt* (1988), *Hedda Gabler* (1994), *A Doll's House* (1997), *The Lady from the Sea* (2008), *Oedipus* (2008), *Helen* (2009), *Ghosts* (2010), *John Gabriel Borkman* (2010), *Damned by Despair* (2012) and *The Dead* (2012).

FRANK McGUINNESS

The Hanging Gardens

faber and faber

First published in 2013
by Faber and Faber Limited
74–77 Great Russell Street
London WC1B 3DA

Typeset by Country Setting, Kingsdown, Kent CT14 8ES
Printed and bound by CPI Group (UK) Ltd, Croydon, CR0 4YY

A CIP record for this book
is available from the British Library

978-0-571-27827-5

2 4 6 8 10 9 7 5 3 1

Characters

Sam Grant
a reclusive novelist

Jane Grant
his wife, a distinguished gardener

Charlie Grant
his elder son

Rachel Grant
his daughter

Maurice Grant
his younger son

The Hanging Gardens was first performed on the Abbey stage of the Abbey Theatre, Dublin, on 9 October 2013. The cast, in alphabetical order, was as follows:

Rachel Grant Cathy Belton
Jane Grant Barbara Brennan
Sam Grant Niall Buggy
Charlie Grant Declan Conlon
Maurice Grant Marty Rea

Director Patrick Mason
Set Design Michael Pavelka
Lighting Design Davy Cunningham
Costume Design Joan O'Clery
Sound Design Denis Clohessy
Voice Director Andrea Ainsworth

THE HANGING GARDENS

For Roisin and Tim

PROLOGUE

Strange music.
   Moonlight, and intense rain.
   In his pyjamas Sam sits on a bench.
   The rain soaks him, to his delight.
   Two figures, dressed in raincoats, wearing wellingtons and carrying large, dark umbrellas, enter.
   Though they are unrecognisable, the pair are Jane and Charlie.
   Sam raises his arms to them.

Sam Fetch me the moon shining on Babylon. Let its gods shower blessings on me. Fetch me diadems of sun and stars. Let me wear this crown of rain, rain that's drenched me.

   He starts to parade about the garden as Rachel and Maurice enter, wearing heavy raincoats and carrying umbrellas.

Charlie Father.

Sam For these lands are my kingdom, my hanging gardens.

Maurice Father.

Sam Not just that house –

   He points in the direction of the house.

Rachel Father.

Sam That house which is Babylon.

Jane Sam.

Sam My palace is Babylon, and you walk in the hanging gardens.

Jane Sam, get in – you're soaked.

He sees Jane.
Jane takes him by the hand.
Charlie shelters him with the umbrella.
They lead Sam inside, leaving Rachel and Maurice in the rain. They follow them inside.
Fade.

SCENE ONE

Birdsong.
  Morning.
  The rain has stopped and sunlight fills the garden.
  Rachel and Maurice are in the garden.
  Rachel is carrying two red bowls of vanilla ice cream,
spoons in each, one for her, one for Maurice.

Rachel A reward for you.

She hands him the bowl of ice cream.
  They start to eat.

You walked to Buncrana and back. The whole of the
White Strand. Meet anybody?

Maurice Couldn't put a name to their faces.

Rachel Were they natives?

Maurice Natives? What do you think we are?

Rachel We never did mingle, not if Mama and Papa had
their way. So, what did they say? Let me guess – 'Young
fella, is that yourself? Aren't you one of the Grant boys?
Have you stopped the learning? How's the sister – still at
the law down in Dublin? Coming home at her age with a
babby in her belly – isn't it great? How are your mammy
and daddy taking it? Broken-hearted – Your daddy, still
writing?'

Maurice He is, yes.

Rachel 'Mammy toiling away in her big garden? How
does that woman do all the work on her own? She's
getting no younger. And the gardens themselves – they

must be the last word. I'd say they're beautiful – from what little can be seen from the side of the road. Will there ever come a time when they let a body set eyes on them?' And that was the end of the conversation.

Maurice Well guessed.

Rachel No guessing at all. We have the same interrogation – even the parents – when they show their faces in the town.

Maurice Don't know the town – not sure I even know the parents. You've had longer to become acquainted –

Rachel Poor wee Maurice, baby of the tribe.

Maurice points to her stomach.

Maurice Not for much longer.

Rachel At least you've noticed, you could manage a congratulations. The one and so far only grandchild – I hope it's not expecting a big welcome. When I told him, my father looked at me as if I were speaking gibberish. Ma coughed –

Maurice What kind? The cough of the broken-hearted or the cough of the martyr? A cough more in sorrow than in anger?

Maurice demonstrates the cough.

Rachel Perfect, or nearly so. You're lacking in one requirement. 'Years of experience. Of serving other people. Husband and children. What would I have done without the gardens – my only pleasure? Did you know they were run wild – a jungle – when I started? I saved them – me – your mother.'

Maurice And you should be acknowledged for that. A bit of credit where credit's due. Not just your father who has the artist's touch.

Rachel No, you have as well, Ma.

Maurice coughs, followed by Rachel.
They burst out laughing.

Rachel God forgive us.

Maurice Shame on you.

Rachel Why? Because there's no God?

Maurice There's no forgiveness.

Rachel Not in this neck of the woods.

Maurice So don't expect it. Who's the father?

Rachel You don't know him.

Maurice Do you?

Rachel I know so many.

Maurice One-night stand?

Rachel Do people still have them?

Maurice You're a very chary lady.

Rachel I've learned to be.

Maurice Just being curious.

Rachel Curiosity killed the cat.

Maurice Lucky cat.

Rachel You're starting to sound like Daddy.

Charlie enters, silencing their conversation.

Charlie Enjoying your ice creams, are you? Making the best of the good weather? Do. Do that. You took your leisurely stroll, I believe? And you, Rachel, sitting humming lullabies to your little bump?

Rachel What's rattled your cage?

Charlie Me? Don't let any thoughts about me enter your pretty heads.

Rachel Then would you ever fetch us some iced tea?

Charlie I am not your dogsbody. If you want iced tea, fetch it yourself.

Rachel I will.

Charlie And while you're at it, fetch him his breakfast. That him is your father, in case you've forgotten. It's simple – all he wants is tea and toast. Three times I've brought that up to him. Three times he's turned his nose up at it. Never touched a bite. Would he write today or not? Would he make a start answering the mountain of mail waiting? Was he going to put on a shirt and pair of trousers? Was he going to sit in his pyjamas all day? No answer. I'm going off my head with him, folks – I'm at the end of my tether. It's the forgetfulness – he keeps on and on not remembering. And my mother, she's still in denial. It's not him I mind as much as I do her – Ma.

Rachel The word thanks was never in her vocabulary.

Charlie She still refuses to hire any man to keep the gardens in shape. And no home help either. They're united on that.

Maurice They're united on everything.

Charlie I dared to bring up the subject of a nurse – get somebody local. And I was bawled out. Not our way. We keep ourselves to ourselves, no matter what it costs to any other people apart from the two of them.

Rachel Somewhere inside him he must be grateful to you, Charlie.

Charlie Sam Grant has always maintained gratitude is the worst of all human vices – take gratitude from no one, show it to no one. Will saying thanks get the job done? Do you know what it takes to write a novel?

Maurice The power to stand on your own two feet. Last as long as the bastard of a book takes. For the book must be finished.

Charlie The book will be finished.

Rachel And when the book is finished, what then?

Maurice Start another one.

Rachel Start immediately.

Charlie And he did – frequently.

Rachel He did always. So, he wrote his books –

Charlie Yes, he did.

Maurice He writes books, acclaimed, awarded prizes –

Rachel But not any more - he writes no more.

Maurice His choice.

Rachel His mind's choice – his body – dying body – dying mind.

Charlie Not yet.

Maurice My father is not dying. Is he, Charlie?

Charlie Not while I'm here.

Maurice Is he, Rachel?

Rachel I can't say, Maurice.

Maurice Say it – say he isn't.

Rachel If Charlie says it, he knows best.

Maurice Still say it.

Rachel He's not dying, my father.

Silence.

Do you know what I might just do today? Offer to do a bit of work in the gardens.

Charlie Ma won't let you near them.

Rachel I want to plant something with her. How about that for a shock to the bold Janey Grant?

Rachel cackles.

Rachel I believe that woman would be happier if I had a bunch of dahlias growing inside me.

Charlie Why dahlias?

Rachel Why not? All right, daffodils – delphiniums. She'd certainly be more interested. Well, Charlie, before I start ploughing the fields, would you like me to make breakfast for our genius, the old shite?

Maurice That's our father you're referring to.

Rachel You stay sweet with him, Maurice – stick up for him. Who knows what he might hand out? You could strike lucky. Well, Charlie, do I make him breakfast?

Charlie When he's said no, he means no. Don't try forcing him. That puts him into a dark mood.

Rachel My father in a dark mood – whatever next?

Maurice You're sure you don't want us to give you a hand?

Charlie Certain. I had my outburst earlier. That's calmed me. I have the day's cooking to prepare, and I'm off to fetch his newspapers.

Rachel Let him get his own papers.

Charlie We can't.

Rachel Why?

Charlie You don't know why we can't?

Rachel shakes her head.

He's started to get lost, just going to the shop. They phone up and tell us he doesn't know the way home. He can't be let out even that far on his own. What if he wandered on to the White Strand? Strayed into Lough Swilly and got drowned? No, I have to get the papers.

Maurice It's as rough as that?

Charlie Rougher. You saw last night - we can handle it. No rest here for the wicked. Be warned. Trust your big brother. He knows how this house runs itself.

Charlie exits and Rachel looks after him, now joined by Maurice.

Rachel And you make sure we know you do, O proud prince of Babylon. Or maybe not. Maybe you are just what you think you are – a living saint.

Maurice Why the sarcasm?

Rachel He lost the head very early this time. Normally it doesn't happen until the end of our excursion north. He paces himself magnificently, I will say that. After all, he learned how to from Da. They know precisely when to lose the head. So, why the spasm? No doubt about it, definitely up to something, our Charlie.

Maurice He says Daddy's getting lost leaving the house.

Rachel I heard – but do I believe him? No, Charlie is up to something, but what? I'm dying to find out. Are you?

Rachel and Maurice exit.

The light is now later in the morning.
Jane does her work, precisely, knowledgeably, even automatically.
This is what she does in the garden, resting little, choosing her own moments of stillness, occasionally letting them be chosen for her, less occasionally humming to herself.
Sam opens the pages of the first newspaper and reads them, scissors in hand.

Sam This heat – unnatural in this place.

Jane Donegal?

Sam Yes. What's the difference between Donegal and Siberia?

Jane Tell me –

Sam You can get a train through Siberia. You can't in Donegal. Shaven heads –

Jane Whose?

Sam Convicts, sent to Siberia, all shaven heads. When did I last get my hair cut?

Jane How would I remember?

Sam Can you not?

Jane You should know better than I do – it's your hair.

Sam Is it too long? Do I look like a savage?

Jane I don't think so. What do you think?

Sam I can't see my own hair.

Jane You could look in a mirror. The effort of that won't kill you.

Sam When did I stop looking in the mirror? Was it when you stopped being a hairdresser? Could there be a connection?

Jane Sorry?

Sam When did you stop cutting hair for a living? It's not today or yesterday.

Jane I never worked as a hairdresser.

Sam I beg to differ, but you did, Jane.

Jane Exactly when? Time and place?

Sam Years ago, when we were courting – in college, in Dublin. That flat in Ranelagh – 69 Moyne Road. Number 69. That dirty room where we first – what was it? You had the bright idea of going into the barber business.

Jane How could you have had a business in that flat? You said yourself it was just one dirty room. You couldn't breathe if there were more than two people in it. It's when we started to keep ourselves to ourselves, two oddballs. Barely big enough for the both of us.

Sam You thought that would be the novelty. All crushed in together, one on top of the other, queuing round the block to get into you. Men dying for your fingers to rub across their scalps. Women as well, wanting you to touch their hair, growing everywhere. Well, you were out of luck. Nobody showed their faces. You kept your scissors to yourself.

Jane Whatever fantasy you're entertaining, the only hair I ever mangled was your own and the children's, when we hadn't a bean.

Sam Where are they?

Jane About the house somewhere, or in the garden.

Sam Are they playing? Are they climbing the trees? Making a house up in the branches?

Jane A bit long in the tooth for that.

Sam Then what do they want?

Jane What do you mean?

Sam Why are they crying?

Jane They're not.

Sam I can hear them. Do you not? Are they looking for something?

Silence.

Do they need their hair cut?

Jane If they do, they can go into Buncrana and pay for it. Will you get it into your skull that I know next to nothing about hairdressing? Only one joke. Shall I tell you it?

Sam If you like. Is it long?

Jane Not that long.

Sam Will you remember the ending? You usually forget the ending.

Jane You can still remember things like that –

Sam Still remember – what do you mean?

Jane Do you want to listen to me or not? A woman goes to get her hair cut –

Sam What colour is it? Her hair?

Jane Red, say –

Sam It's important, because that will settle what she wears.

Jane A red-haired woman wearing blue goes to get her hair –

Sam What length was it before cutting?

Jane Quite long – she just wants a trim.

Sam Is she related to the hairdresser?

Jane Cousins.

Sam So they both have the family red hair – useful.

Jane A red-haired woman wearing blue goes to her cousin, also wearing blue, to get her hair trimmed –

Sam Much better. Now we have a family, a rivalry, a purpose –

Jane Sam, I'm telling you a funny story. It's a joke – one voice only, please. May I fire away without any more interruptions?

Sam Or you'll forget the ending? Do I already know the ending?

Jane You don't.

Sam So you haven't already told me this?

Jane I don't believe so.

Sam Then don't expect me to bail you out when you can't remember where this is leading to, because I don't know how to, unless I can guess. Do you think I will be able to guess?

Jane You might be.

Sam Then don't bother telling me if I know what you're going to say in the first place. I have better things to do than listen to your jokes.

Jane Such as?

Silence.

What better things have you to do, Sam?

Silence.

May I proceed?

Sam What's stopping you?

Jane You are politeness itself, sir.

Sam The woman's hair must be cut by now.

Jane So the hairdresser asks the usual question. Where are you going on your holidays? Rome, the woman says. Rome – no, no, no, the hairdresser answers. Rome's desperate, awful, go somewhere else – Rome is smelly, the food's disgusting, the people filthy. Not Rome. Who are you flying with? Ryanair, the woman answers. Ryanair – no, no, no, the hairdresser tells her. Desperate, awful – Ryanair, fly someone else. Always late, fly miles from where you think you're going, costs a fortune when all the extras are added on. Not Ryanair. Why are you going to Rome anyway? To see the Pope, the woman says. The Pope – no, no, no. In St Peter's Square? Desperate, awful, packed with people, you'll never see him. Take my advice, go somewhere else. But the woman does go and comes back a week later. Who does she bump into but the hairdresser. Well, how was Rome? Terrific, food lovely, very clean city. Ryanair? Terrific, left on time, landed near Rome, lovely staff. And the Pope – did you see him in St Peter's Square? Not merely did I see him, the woman says, when he was being carried on

24

his chair through the throng, didn't he stop and beckon me over. He singled me out for some reason, so I knelt down to get his blessing. He put his hands on my shoulders, he looked straight into my face, he said to me, 'Where did you get your hair done? No, no, no – it's desperate, awful, go somewhere else.'

Sam And did she?

Jane What?

Sam Go to another hairdresser's? Was there a second one in the town? Did it cause a family rift? I want to know how it ends, the story.

Jane It's a joke, not a story. It's just meant to be funny.

Sam It doesn't ring true. Can I change it?

Jane Be my guest.

Sam A woman goes to Rome – an old woman. She travels alone.

Jane Why alone?

Sam Her husband's left her, or her husband's died. Not sure yet. For some reason she wants to see the Pope.

Jane She believes in the Pope?

Sam Wants his blessing. The blessing, she believes, will bring her beauty back –

Jane Bring back her husband?

Sam So she believes, or she says so. There will be a miracle in St Peter's Square. She joins the crowd, and he passes, the Pope. When she looks at him, she sees he has the face of a dead man –

Jane A skeleton?

Sam A face fat with bones, bones she knows, she has touched, bones of her lover that the Pope now guards, turning them into – word – word – what is the word?

Jane A relic?

Sam A relic, perhaps – that he raises in benediction. With the tip of the relic he touches her head and her hair – her red hair whitens – stiffens – turns to ice. On this day in Rome where the heat could raise blisters on your back, a woman froze to the bone as if there was inside her some kind of tundra –

Jane And can nothing save her?

Sam Nothing – nothing can bring her back – bring her red hair back – and she dies from grief. Does that ring true or not? This story – is it dead on its feet, wandering, going nowhere? I'm asking you, Jane. Should I ask the hairdresser? Should I ask the Pope? Which Pope could tell me? How about John? John XXIII. Wee Pope John, years ago.

Sam starts reciting a parody of the song 'Big Bad John'.

Sam
Every morning round about a quarter to eight
You can see him arrive at the Vatican gate.
He's short, he's fat, he's bald in the head,
Every other cardinal wishes he was dead –
He's John – Pope Joooohn – wee Pope John.

They laugh.

Sam And he did die. After him I stopped taking any notice of that palaver. A shower of heathens, that's what this town calls us. So be it, heathens we'll stay. Call this house Babylon, cultivate the hanging gardens, where we worship – who is it we worship, Jane?

26

Jane Nobody, Sam. And the hanging gardens are your description. You yourself called our house Babylon. We worship nobody.

Sam I know who you'd like to worship. The queue of men, their tongues hanging out, waiting for you in your fancy barbershop –

Jane For the last time, I did not –

Sam Are you going to hit me?

Silence.

Are you going to hit me?

She sits down.

Jane I am not going to hit you – no.

Silence.

What makes you think I would hit you?

Sam Did we ever beat the children?

Jane We might have been tempted, but I don't think we did.

Sam Should we have beaten them?

Jane Maybe. No – no – no, we should not have. Are you all right now?

Sam Should I not be?

Jane Why should you not?

Sam Jane, I'm looking at you and I have something to tell you.

Jane Which is?

Sam You'd be a fine-looking woman if you'd stop turning into a tree or a bush, or whatever it is you're planting.

He touches her cheek bones.

Sam Those bones – still my magnificent Jew.

Jane Sam, my granny got lost coming off a boat from Latvia. The silly bitch thought Belfast was Boston and stayed. She learned to keep quiet about who she was when she learned English, until she revealed all only on her deathbed, crying out for a rabbi in Yiddish.

Sam And did he come?

Jane Ireland's not overrun by rabbis then or now. She died alone. My mother blessed her as best she could, singing some of her old songs. There's the story I was taught, and that's how much of a Jew I am, as you well know.

Sam I mean it – magnificent, if you'd do something about yourself.

Jane What would you suggest?

Sam Take a holiday. Far away from me. From the gardens. We'll still be here when you come back.

Jane What makes you think I would come back?

Sam You couldn't stay away.

Jane From you? From the gardens?

Sam You are the gardens. And me, what am I? You can see what I am from what's in front of you.

Jane Would you not go back to the world, Sam?

Sam What world?

Jane Writing.

Sam Why?

Jane The books – wonderful stories.

Sam We don't need the money. You made your pile with your how-to-garden shite. You worked hard at it. You deserve all you get. What need have we of the world? Where would we go? New York? Falling down. London? Finished. Dublin? Poisonous. Falling – finished – poisonous – them, or me? Maybe we should trek to Latvia. Find this rabbi to convert us –

Jane I'm sure he did a runner years ago. Why did you lose such faith in people?

Sam People let you down. They don't intend to, but they do. They've been let down themselves that often, it's now so deep in their nature, they have to. Trust no one. I should know that – I was one of them for long enough.

Jane No regrets letting it go?

Sam They let me go. And nothing could save me, dead on my feet, or just wandering, going nowhere, nobody knowing where I'm heading.

Jane They never stop wanting you back.

Sam A lie you tell to comfort me. No lies. No comfort. Not in that business. Books. Best out of it. Writing. Well out of it. Let it go. And it's gone. It will never come back. What grief.

Silence.

Grief.

Silence.

The grief, Jane. Get over it. We have each other.

Jane And the children. The three of them.

Sam Four. We have four children.

Jane Not at last count, Sam. There's our daughter, Rachel. Our sons, Charlie and Maurice. That makes three, unless I've been counting wrong for years.

Sam Are you not including the other one?

Jane Which other one – what are you talking about?

Sam I know we had another one. Sometimes she comes and talks to me. Why are you denying her?

Jane Because she does not exist. She's not here.

Sam I think she is –

Jane Sam, I've put up with a lot, but this – I am putting the record straight on this here and now. We have one daughter – no other –

Sam I know what's behind this. Why you reject her. She was born black, wasn't she? You couldn't face that.

Jane How could we two have a black child?

Sam Maybe she was born dead?

Jane We never had a black daughter.

Sam I said a dead daughter – stillborn.

Jane We never had a stillborn baby. No daughter of ours died – are you clear on that?

Sam begins to tear newspapers, slowly, methodically.

Sam Are you dead and buried? Were you eating your dinner when a restaurant exploded? Were you shot in the belly one Sunday, running, squealing from the soldiers? Did you cry, Mammy, Daddy, save me? Did your flesh turn black in a blaze, a wreath of poppies in your hand?

He continues slowly, methodically, to tear the newspaper pages.

Did you give water to a dying boy – and get a bullet in the head for doing that? Are you lying somewhere in the sands, waiting to be found, waiting to be let go, lost across the border?

Jane We lost no one.

Sam Or maybe you pulled the trigger – she pulled the trigger on a woman weeping for mercy – maybe that's who's missing.

He stops tearing the pages of the newspaper and starts to search through the torn pages.

Jane Sam, I can't handle this turn of events.

Sam I understand that you're in denial. Your heart must be broken, but it's better to admit things. Get them out into the open. Tell your story.

Jane Sam, look me in the face – who am I?

He stops searching.

This is all a dream to you, nothing but –

Sam My daughter is a dream?

Jane She does not exist. She was never born. There is no such child.

Sam Then why does she talk to me? She whispers all the time. I do see her. I'll prove it to you. I'll find her.

He gets up to go search.
She holds him back as they wrestle.

Jane Stop this – she is not here. She never has been.

Sam Someone missing – they always are, after a war –
I must find them – will you stop me searching –

Jane That war has stopped.

Sam It will never stop till no one's left to search – till no
one's here –

Jane Your family are all here. I'm here – you are too.
Rachel – Charlie – Charlie – Maurice. Show yourself to
your father.

*He punches her hard in the stomach and she doubles
up in pain.*
He runs off.
Jane slowly recovers to her feet.

Patience, give me patience.

The strange music recurs, and fade.

SCENE THREE

Birdsong.
The light changes to afternoon.
*Sam is now lying on his back on the lawn, his hands
raised as if conducting the birds.*
Maurice enters.
Sam ignores him.

Maurice Charlie says lunch is getting cold. Are you on
hunger strike? I'm sent to get you.

Silence.

She's worried, Ma is. Could you not humour her and
step inside? What's keeping you out?

Silence.

Are you looking for something here?

Sam Who is it you are again?

Maurice You know bloody well who I am, Daddy. You knew this morning. Don't tell me you've forgotten in the space of a few hours.

Sam A lot can happen in that time.

Sam sits up on the lawn.

Maurice Even more can't.

Sam What does not happen, what cannot happen, is that what interests you? Yes, I now place you in the scheme of things. The brainy one, took years to finish college. What's become of you? Did you go into teaching?

Maurice I left it.

Sam What were you teaching?

Maurice Philosophy – lecturing in philosophy. Well, giving tutorials, trying to get a full-time job in college –

Sam A good philosopher.

Sam rises from the ground.

That's how my old boy used to describe me, when he saw fit to dismiss the books I wrote. That's if he ever took time to read a word of them, slogging in his huckster of a drapery shop, looking down on the world that had no arse in its trousers. He'd seen them all changing their drawers behind his curtains, making him his living, giving me a schooling. All he was ever proud of was that the same schooling beat the brogue out of me. Everything else was of no matter. In that respect, you resemble me. Our fathers both thought us useless.

Maurice That's what you make of me?

33

Sam What I make of you all. Why did you leave teaching?

Maurice Travelling – learning about the world – learning about myself - seeing Asia and Africa – picking up bits and pieces of languages – nearly settled in Spain - doing what I should have done after my degree, instead of running into a doctorate –

Sam On what?

Maurice Semantics – words – how we never mean what we say –

Sam I do. I mean what I say. So you turned your back on school books?

Maurice They were driving me to an early grave.

Sam Is there such a thing?

Maurice I don't follow –

Sam It's a philosophical speculation – such a thing as an *early* grave? Is it not just a release?

Maurice The grave?

Sam Well, what do you think?

Maurice We could argue the toss better inside. Will you not come in?

Sam Why come back here? What are you looking for? Is it to bail out the poor old ma and da?

Maurice Ma can't keep on doing all the work by herself –

Sam She has, up till now.

Maurice She's looking tired.

Sam That's because she has so much work to do – so much extra work – now that I'm not the man I used to be. All that worry, minding me.

Maurice I didn't say that.

34

Sam You didn't have to. Yes – I remember you now exactly. Always and ever running away. Never settling. Now you can break the habit of a lifetime. Make my mind up for me. What should I do? You, resolve what's best. Put me away. Put me down. Put me out of my misery. It's what you're all here to settle. And I know who's behind it. Your beloved mother. Did she not ask you to come home?

Maurice I swear she didn't. Rachel and myself arrived together by chance –

Sam Do you still go in for blackmail?

Silence.

Blackmail. The photographs. You must remember, how could you forget?

Silence.

You, in women's underwear. You, wanking to your heart's content.

Sam laughs.

Do you think I wouldn't know who sent them to me, the photographs?

Silence.

You did, you yourself. I've waited for years to ask you why you did that? Did you want me to show them to your mother? Or was it for me to notice you?

Maurice Yes, it was, Father.

Sam Well, now I have. Are you happy that's so? What did you expect from me exactly? Don't tell me that it was pity. I despise pity –

Maurice So do I –

Sam Then what were you looking for?

35

Maurice You to help me.

Sam And I did – by doing nothing. No tears – no screaming match – no blaming anyone. Aren't you better off neglected?

Maurice I was not – we were not neglected –

Sam Maybe you were. Maybe we might have been more careful. We must have seen signs. You played a girl in that school concert. What possessed us to allow you? Do you remember?

Sam sings in his own voice.

Sam
   The sun, whose rays
   Are all ablaze
   With ever-living glory,
   Does not deny
   His majesty,
   He scorns to tell a story.

Maurice sings in his adult voice.

Maurice
   Observe his flame,
   That placid dame,
   The moon's Celestial Highness;
   And, truth to tell,
   She lights up well,
   So I, for one, don't blame her!

Sam joins in with Maurice.

Sam/Maurice
   Ah, pray make no mistake,
   We are not shy.
   We're very wide awake,
   The moon and I!

Sam How troubling – how beautiful – becoming a Japanese girl. It was your triumph. Who could believe you were a boy? Dressed in that strange kimono, happy, your face at peace beneath all that white make-up. So convincing. I wondered what we were doing. What happened to you?

Maurice My voice broke.

Sam And have you not got over it?

Maurice I can't tell you that.

Sam Why not?

Maurice Because I'm not sure who I am.

Silence, as Rachel enters, unseen by Maurice and Sam.

I don't know.

Sam It's time you learned.

Maurice Who'll teach me? You?

Sam One day standing in the toilet, I thought I'd lost my cock. I was looking for it everywhere. Guess where it was? Lost in my kimono – buried in my underpants. Would you have helped me find it? Do I frighten you?

Silence.

That father I was telling you about – my father –

Maurice He died when I was little –

Sam I thought him a fool right up until the end when he went – he went adrift – that's the word. He started not to believe all he'd ever put faith in. Yes, he took strange, as they say. And what started it? The moon landing. He started to declare that if they found life there, he'd stop believing in God. They didn't – and he did, stop that is. Never went to Mass again. Barely left the shop.

Maintained the moon was in the house. And the furniture we'd had for years, he claimed that at night, it started barking. Chairs, table, beds and mats. One night he made a bonfire of the carpets – took a hatchet and smashed our bits and pieces to smithereens. That would warn the moon. Mad a little – mad a lot – in some lunar trance – lunar, luna, lunatic. Yes, he frightened me, in case I should become what he are –

Maurice Is – was.

Silence.

What he was.

Sam What I am. What you might be. What you are. Am I to tell you what you are? Is it not time you told me?

Silence as Sam sees Rachel.

You should never give anything away.

Rachel Away about what?

Sam That would be telling, wouldn't it, Maurice? And I would never do that, would I, daughter?

Maurice exits.

Rachel What's got into him? What the hell have you said to him?

Sam What else but fatherly advice? Some home truths, that's all.

Rachel You could listen to a few of those yourself.

Sam Are you going to deliver them?

Rachel Why – would you listen to me?

Sam A first time for everything?

Rachel Not for that, Da – never for that.

Sam Why are you so sure?

Rachel We never change – we're too alike, Father.

Sam Even though you might not be mine?

Rachel laughs.

Rachel You are slipping up, Papa. That was the line of attack you used to keep for Christmas night in the horrors of the brandy. I laughed in your face when you first tried it. I believe I passed that little test. You approved of my cruelty. You were rearing me right. If I could cope with you, I could cope with anybody or anything.

He points at her belly.

Sam Is that how you'll rear the bundle of joy?

Rachel pats her belly.

Rachel My little miracle? My business, strictly my own work. No, not quite true. I let science do its bit. Could you beat that? It knocks the Angel Gabriel into the corner.

Sam I think you'll find the Holy Ghost did the business in that quarter, my learned friend.

Rachel Such theological exactness, my lord. But then you have the kind of knowledge there that we lack. You did make sure we were spared all religious cant –

Sam You did well without battling against those mad bastards –

Rachel All we had to battle against was your madness.

Sam I trust you won't exclude your mother from the asylum.

Rachel An unfortunate choice of location, in the circumstances.

Sam Appropriate, though – for her or for me? Asylum – is that what's on the cards?

Silence.

I could always talk you into shooting your mouth off. Maybe that's useful for a barrister. Is it a help in family cases, such as should the likes of me be committed?

Silence.

Is that where you see me heading? In your learned, legal opinion would you lead me there and lock me up? Is that how my fine daughter the barrister ends up excelling – shoving her da in the mental home?

Silence.

Am I not still sharp as a razor, seeing it all as distinctly as I do? Are you still as sharp as a razor, lady? Do you know what is actually occurring here? Do you notice her as closely as you've been observing me? Or have the warnings to keep the old man under scrutiny let her off the hook, as she always has been? She's more quiet then I am. She does keep herself more busy. And she's so very worried about me. Me, your father. Yet she's the one losing it. Have you not got sign of that? She's slipping.

Rachel In what way slipping?

Sam Have you actually been talking to her? Is she all excited about the fruit of your womb? Is she making plans for you?

Rachel She's barely mentioned it.

Sam Do you know why?

Rachel We're not that kind – we keep our distance.

Sam Her daughter is pregnant with her first grandchild. There's keeping your distance and there's dementia. The bitch is more interested in her trees than in her own. Her hard heart is cut from wood. There's times I believe I would have been better off marrying a horse chestnut. Has it not dawned on you why she shows no concern for you? Do you know?

Rachel I know that woman. I know she'd die for us. Die for me. She just has no way of showing it – no more than I have of showing her how much I – how much –

   Silence.

Hard beings, silent on certain subjects, each of us our mother's daughters, secrets passed in the blood, from one woman in this family down through each and every one, ready for battle, which is just as well, considering the men surrounding them.

Sam She imagines it's hers, the child. That's what she whispers to me, under her breath, in the dark of the night. She's convinced it's swelling inside her, not you. And if you want more proof she's losing the plot, wait for this little surprise. She tells me the baby is black. She's going to give birth to a black man's son or daughter. She thinks she's been off seeing Asia and Africa, picking up bits and pieces of languages, picking up men, she imagines, thinking she's having a baby, not you.

   Silence.

Nothing to say to that, have you? You don't believe me, do you? I'm lying, am I?

   Silence.

Or is my mind gone completely?

Rachel It's your mind – you still know that, Daddy.

41

Sam Do you know yours? Do you want the house? Is that your dream? You're back to get your share before Charlie cleans up. He gets us to sign it all over to him when we are both doting. He's not as green as he's cabbage-looking. Weed him out. Get yourself installed. Get your share – the lion's share. She'll give it to him – he was always her boy, Charlie, a bit slower than the other two, more in need of minding. Am I right or am I wrong?

Rachel Da, there are times you are very right, and times you are very wrong.

Sam Which is which this time, would you say?

Rachel I'll keep my eyes and ears open – I'll let you know.

Sam Do that. Look, listen and learn. You're the smart girl. Always have been. Capable of standing on your own two feet – getting what you want. Isn't the child evidence of that? The whole business – it must have set you back a few bob.

Rachel It wasn't cheap.

Charlie enters, unseen by Sam and Rachel.

Sam You managed.

Rachel I just about managed. There were a few false –

Sam Hopes?

Rachel Hopes, yes.

Sam Brave girl. Why do it?

Rachel What I saw – in the family courts.

Sam You had a heart hard enough for it. What you saw in this house –

Rachel Was nothing to what I witnessed there. Christ knows, you two were not perfect, but you never led us down the corridors of that courthouse and left us there. Maybe at least I could match you in that. So I'd give it a go, the baby, while I still had some chance. Brave girl, you say? Broke girl. I've spent what I had on the treatment.

Sam You never asked us for a penny?

Rachel I knew better.

Sam Fair enough.

Rachel I think so too – fair as it could be.

Sam You don't worry not knowing its father?

Rachel starts to laugh.

You do know the father?

Rachel I know my father – that's why I'm smiling. You let me in on the joke, even if you couldn't see it yourself.

Sam Would I die for you – like your mother?

Rachel You'd kill for us.

Sam I'm not sure that's a compliment.

Rachel It isn't.

Sam sees Charlie.

Sam Rachel here tells me she sees me as a bit of a laugh. A joke. What do you say to that, Charlie? Would you agree? Do I leave you bursting your sides?

Charlie Come in, Da, eat.

Rachel Sound advice, Father. Home truths, as you've said. You're next in line, Charlie. Myself and Maurice have been on the receiving end of his wit and wisdom. I wonder what he'll pass on to you.

43

Rachel exits.

Charlie Pass on what to me? What is she talking about?

Sam Don't fret, Charlie. I've given nothing away. So you're out here to force me in as well?

Charlie Ma wants you inside, and yes, so do I. Come and eat.

Sam I'm the popular man.

Charlie We might make a start on the mountain of mail waiting for you.

Sam A mountain, you always say – definitely I'm a popular fellow.

Charlie They've taken the bother of writing to you –

Sam Have I asked them to?

Charlie You owe them some sort of reply.

Sam Replies you want? All right. Anybody offering honours – refuse. Anybody wanting film or TV rights, the books stay what they are – books. Anybody asking the meaning of anything, put straight into the bin. Anybody looking for money – do they still look for money? – a polite but firm refusal. No stamp on the answering envelope. What makes people think that cash grows on these trees? Why do they believe that?

Charlie They take one look at this big lump, living off his parents, draining them dry, me the lazy bollocks who can never take the hint it might be time to do a runner and see the world. Could you put it better yourself, Da, from your poisonous lips?

Silence.

I wait on you morning, noon and night. You want for nothing if I can provide it. You bellow, you bark – I do as you demand. Am I the worst in the world for having done so? Will you not acknowledge I do my best?

Silence.

No – no answer to that. No reply in return. What I get in return is bed and board. Not much else. You have no thanks, do you? What you give me back is sharper than no thanks. I serve you, and you hate me for it. Father, I believe you hate me.

Sam Hate?

Charlie I say hate –

Sam And I ask is it you who hates me?

Silence.

Do you hear what I'm asking?

Charlie nods.

Might I have done what you say so that you could hate me?

Charlie I don't understand you. You're my father. Why do that?

Sam So you would love her more.

Charlie My mother?

Sam And you do love her, don't you?

Charlie Of course I do.

Sam Why?

Charlie She's my mother, isn't she?

Sam And she lets you love her, doesn't she? But I don't let you love me. Why?

Silence.

Is it because of her? I let her have all your love – I always have – because she needs it more. She demands it.

Charlie Demands?

Sam Your mother gets what she wants, doesn't she? When she puts her mind to something, it gets done. These gardens – what would they be without her fierce work?

Charlie A wilderness.

Sam That's what it was like when you were a youngster, do you recall?

Charlie A bit.

Sam Sheer hard toil – that's what made them what they are now. Give her credit where it's due – one of the best in the whole country. She knows what's what, and we know the murderous effort goes into their keep. She rules the roost. The woman's will of iron. Just as well she has, she's needed it. To manage me. Is that right?

Silence.

And she has a temper to match that will of iron. Do you remember that temper when you were a little boy?

Charlie laughs.

Charlie She could lose the rag, yes.

Sam The rag, the bone, the whole damn shop. And it was you who provoked her. More you than the other two desperadoes. You were the beloved, the first born. All mistakes are made there.

Charlie How so?

Sam A right little villain.

Charlie What did I do?

Sam You knew exactly what to do.

Charlie What the hell did I do?

Sam Picked bare every flower – every rose, every lupin – her dahlias, her pride and joy – you plucked them clean into a box and showered them at her feet. It was like a river of red petals. She just lost control – completely lost control with you.

Charlie I don't remember her that hot-headed.

Sam A woman of fierce temper. Or iron will, as you agree. A violent woman.

Charlie That is nonsense.

Sam So you have no memory of it?

Charlie Memory of what?

Sam Me, restraining that mad woman from harming you?

Silence.

Her fists across your face. You kick her in the shins. That drives her insane. Can you not see her rage?

Silence.

You crying for me to save you. Do you not remember?

Charlie I remember crying not to be put to bed –

Sam Naked in my arms. She stripped you of every stitch. Who were you crying to?

Charlie You – I think it was you.

Sam So I was there for sure?

Charlie Yes, you were.

Sam Carrying you away from her. And you weren't frightened of me?

Charlie No.

Sam Frightened of her, I'm frightened, Charlie –

Charlie Who of?

Sam Who do you think?

Charlie Are you talking about my mother?

Sam Aren't you frightened? I am.

Charlie How?

Sam A violent woman.

Charlie She is not.

Sam A woman of fierce temper – a savage. Against me, she's raised her fist –

Charlie Not true, Da – that cannot be true.

Sam I have never complained about her.

Charlie There is nothing to complain –

Sam She beats me – she did so today. She marks me where it can't be seen – you know to where I am referring. And it is my fault, I let her. I've said nothing against her. And I have to trust you will say nothing. I do trust you, Charlie. Do you me?

Charlie Why would I not have seen any of this?

Sam She makes sure you don't, and so do I.

Charlie Why would my mother do that?

Sam She's suffering, Charlie. A bit adrift, taking strange, that's how some describe it. It's an illness, and it's starting to affect her. I can't go into that house because I'm not safe any more.

Charlie This is madness.

Sam So I am a madman?

Charlie I think you are, Father.

Sam And you, what are you? Do you know what you are?

Charlie I do my best, Daddy, as I've said, and I think you are very ill.

Sam You do, and that's why you mind me. What should be your reward for that – for doing your best? Tell me. What do you think you should receive?

Silence.

What do you think you deserve?

Silence.

Is it the house – the whole kingdom? Babylon and all its gods? Do you call on Bal and Anu to bless you? Aja and Ishtar, greatest goddess? What should they give you? Do you want this house and the hanging gardens? Is that what you ask for?

Charlie Yes.

Sam Should I summon the spirits to rise and anoint you, next in line to me, next to rule in Babylon? Would you like that?

Charlie Yes.

Sam Then believe me.

Sam kisses Charlie on the forehead and holds him in his arms.

49

At long last, you are my son. Now you're mine – not hers, yes?

Charlie embraces Sam back and starts to weep lowly.

Charlie You say you don't let me love you, but I do, Daddy, I love you so very much. I'm really proud of you. Please stop talking the way you just have been. I want you to get well again. I want my daddy back. We all want that. Honest to God, because we don't know what else to do. And I'm sorry for crying.

Sam You should go up to your bed now. Good boy, stop crying. Go to bed. It's early evening – there's still light. No fear of the dark. Don't be afraid. I'll save you. You're a grown fellow now. Enough of this weeping. Enough.

He kisses Charlie.
Charlie exits.

No – weep. Weep your fill. Weep for the fall of Babylon, for all in it. Weep for your father who knows not what he does. Yes, no, I do – or do I?

Jane enters.
Sam starts to walk along the gravel paths of the garden, finding his own pace.

Jane Are you pitching camp here for the evening?

Silence as he keeps walking,

Speak up – I can't hear you.

He keeps silent as he walks.

Will you stand still?

He continues to walk in silence.

I'm not standing arguing with you.

Sam Then go into your house.

Jane Your house as well.

Sam My house? My gardens? I don't want them. I give them back to you.

Jane And I do not take them.

Sam Give them away.

Jane Who to?

Sam Who else? The children.

Jane What if they don't want them?

Sam laughs as he walks by her, never stopping walking.

Sam Not want them? Is that what you say? Their tongues are hanging out – they can't wait –

Jane For us to die?

Sam For me to die.

Jane And do you think that's what's going to happen? How are you going to die?

Sam Exhaustion.

Jane grabs Sam.

Jane But you've been doing nothing.

He stops walking.

Nothing.

Silence.

Nothing for too long. You stopped working.

He starts walking again.

That's what's driven you distracted. The lack of something to do. Except torture me. Torture your children. Are you proud you can do that? Are you happy?

He keeps walking in silence.

You think you're going to die?

Sam Tell me what difference would it make if I did?

Jane Walk on then. Walk away. Walk yourself into the exhaustion you claim will kill you. If you want to die, die. Die.

Jane exits.
Sam stops walking.

Sam Then it's true. She's ordered it.

Sam starts to laugh.

Die.

The laughter grows silent.
He starts to beat the ground with his feet.

Die. Die. Die.

Birdsong is heard.

Birds of the air, tell me a story – save me.

The birdsong intensifies, mixing with the strange music.

Once upon a time – save me.

Fade.

SCENE FOUR

It is now early evening light.
Jane is working alone in the garden.
She fingers a plant gently.
Then, expertly, she locates a dying one and removes it immediately from the soil, tearing it apart with more than necessary ferocity, discarding it on the pathway.

She sees Rachel enter.
Ignoring her, Jane returns to her work.

Rachel He's asking for you. We can't get him to settle down. You might make a better fist of it than we have.

Silence as Jane keeps working.

Rachel Are *you* now refusing to come in?

Jane Let Charlie deal with it.

Rachel Charlie has done a runner.

Jane Where's he gone to?

Rachel Do you need three guesses?

Jane That's perfect – that's all we need. He hasn't the money to go on a bender. Still, better send Maurice to fetch him home.

Rachel Maurice is needed here. He's sitting with my father.

Jane He'll never manage him.

Rachel Then will you come in and at least see if you can put him to his bed?

Jane It's too early. If he sleeps now, he'll be awake all night, rousing the house.

Rachel How long can this go on? How long before you admit he needs treatment?

Jane I don't like the word treatment. I can look after him better than any –

Rachel No, you can't.

Jane I cannot bear the thought of a home – Charlie and myself –

Rachel Can't handle it any more.

Jane Can we afford it? How will we, out of his royalties?

Rachel I'm thinking of your own, Ma. You've made a fortune. Your books make serious dough.

Jane The 'how-to-garden shite'? That was one of his more polite comments.

Rachel I know he looked down his nose at how many you sold, but that's not the point. I'm asking has it all disappeared?

Jane No. No. We live frugally. I'm as I ever was – able to make a pound go a long way. A home – would he stay there? I really don't think we can pay –

Rachel You must have enough money –

Jane But that's needed.

Rachel For what?

Jane The house. The gardens. They are his monument.

Rachel They're yours.

Jane All right, they belong to us both. And we need every penny to make sure they survive as we intend them to. Nothing – no one – can get in the way of that, including the welfare of him or myself. There we agree completely, myself and your father.

Rachel No matter who goes under –

Jane Nobody goes under. We see to that.

Rachel The ever-loving couple.

Jane Do you think so? Are you happy for us?

Rachel No.

Jane Were you ever happy?

54

Rachel No.

Jane Why didn't you tell us?

Rachel You wouldn't have listened.

Jane So you chose not to?

Rachel You couldn't hear me, either of you.

Jane Are you saying we never made time for you? No – not so. You never gave me a minute's peace listening to all your plans. What have they come to? A degree in law. A few years' practice at the bar. Not much to show for that. So what did you do –

Rachel I got away from you.

Jane And you come back. Why?

Rachel I've done a course in copyright law. Intellectual property. I might be some use in dealing with rights. Things are getting more and more complicated –

Jane Stop skirting the issue. Why are you here?

Rachel To depend on you.

Silence.

To depend on you and Daddy. All I've ever learned in life –

Jane I reared you to be the opposite –

Rachel You reared nobody. You planted a bloody garden. You mended a run-down house. Everything else – an inconvenience. That's what Da's become – another inconvenience. And perhaps you won't nurse him. Why should I believe you would? When push comes to shove, you are a thoroughly nasty woman. What have I ever done? I've told my mother she is a dangerous piece of work. And she is all her own making.

55

Jane And you think this shocks me?

Rachel Yes, I think it does.

Jane Well, does this shock you? Leave the house. Get out.

Silence.

Jane No, that's not part of the plot, is it, Rachel?

Silence.

Your child inherits everything. The fresh start. Am I right? The unborn baby. We will melt when we see the beautiful child. That will not come to pass.

Rachel I didn't imagine that it would.

Jane I'm glad you're not slipping.

Rachel I want this child.

Jane And you'll get what you want – to rear it here?

Rachel Yes.

Jane We'll have no say in that then – you just made up your mind? Do everything your way, or no way? I never bought that, Rachel. Still don't. Poor timing. Made your move too quickly. But you always do. Part of your charm, perhaps, but it is a little well-worn, wouldn't you say?

Rachel Then I'm not wanted?

Jane Stop acting the martyr. You've asked, so you'll get what you want. But don't try to rule the roost. One thing I make very clear. I still have the say where your father goes.

Rachel Where does he go?

Jane I don't know.

Rachel Will we be able to cope?

56

Jane I don't know.

Rachel Will you let us help?

Jane The three of you, running rings around me - driving me as mad as your father? Have the two of us committed, and –

Rachel Ma, keep your mouth shut.

Jane Your father's coming?

Rachel No – it's Charlie.

Jane Drunk?

Rachel Walking slowly and carefully – watching himself, not putting a foot wrong.

Jane That drunk? Then we're in for a lecture.

Rachel All I've been getting today.

Jane All you deserve to get.

Rachel Is it?

Charlie enters, having had a few drinks, but he is more sober than Jane thinks.
He walks directly to Jane.

Jane You have the stride of a man who knows where exactly he's going.

Charlie Maybe that's because this man knows exactly what he wants. I want my share.

Rachel Of what?

Charlie The lot. My share. To be paid a fair wage. What's owed to me. That's what I want – what I demand.

Rachel How will you get that?

Charlie Not your business.

He points to Jane.

It's hers. Isn't it, Mother? Only you and Da, only you can give me what I deserve. And I want it immediately. What am I but your beast of burden? Well, I am no beast and I'm dropping my burden. I'm finished with the lot of you. But I won't go quietly. You heard what I said –

Jane Your share - how much precisely?

Silence.

If you are so insistent, I presume you have an exact amount you expect to be handed over.

Charlie My fair share. The same as the rest –

Jane You've not decided on an amount then? You and Rachel and Maurice –

Charlie Rachel and Maurice are not my business. They have not given you their life, as I have.

Jane I did not ask for your life. Neither did your father. And you know that.

Charlie What would you have done without me?

Jane What would you have done without us?

Charlie Gone under.

Silence.

Gone under. That's all I'm fit for – the stupid one. Take it out on me. I tore the heads from your flowers. Ripped the petals off, one by lovely one. I destroyed your garden, and you beat me. Beat me till my legs bled and father dragged you away from me. He saved me, his son, from you, my mother.

Jane Charlie, you really are your father's son.

Charlie How?

Jane You believe your own stories.

Charlie This did happen.

Jane You're thinking of when I tried to trim your hair. Screamed the house down. I snipped your ear by pure accident. A wee bit of blood, nothing more. You'd think I'd stabbed you – your father roaring, I'd damaged his first born. He took you in his arms and carried you to the bathroom to wash the ear clean.

Jane rubs his head and caresses his ear.

A wee bit of blood, nothing more. It would soon have stopped anyway. There's no need to be in pain.

Charlie But I am. I am always.

Jane You only imagine it. Would you not say so, Rachel?

Rachel I say your heart is sore, Charlie. Sorer than I imagined.

Charlie Did you ever in your life, lady, give me a second thought?

Rachel I think I did.

Charlie If you did, it was to point at me, the thicko, doing the donkey work. Donkey Charlie. And you, getting everything –

Rachel It wasn't enough.

Charlie It was more than I had.

Rachel It was never enough.

Charlie And soon you will have what I'd most love, and will never, ever get.

Rachel The baby?

Charlie Does that amaze you? Does that not make you burst your sides? I would love to be a father.

Rachel Who says you won't be?

Charlie bursts out laughing.

Charlie You are a cruel bitch. Tell her why, Ma.

Jane I don't know what it is I've to tell.

Charlie There is only one father in this house. And he rules – Master Sam. He is in complete command. Isn't that correct, Mother?

Jane Aren't you full of questions today, Charlie? I've only one for you. I've asked it before – how much? Is any amount enough? Or, as she says, would nothing ever be enough?

Silence.

How do I get this money that will never be enough? Sell the house. Or sell the gardens.

Silence.

Should I sell both?

Rachel Never.

Jane Should I sell either?

Charlie Never.

Jane Then how do I pay you, Charlie?

Charlie Kick the other two out. Make me the only one. Let us live as we've always lived, me, you and Da.

Rachel Will you let him blackmail you?

Charlie No blackmail – just the way it works best. Do you want her squawking infant distracting your work in the garden?

Rachel This comes from the cretin that wants to be a father.

Charlie You fall for anything, don't you, Rachel? Anything – anyone. That's how you're up the spout.

Jane And I wonder why I prefer plants to human beings. Look, here comes Maurice – what is it you bring to torment your mother?

Maurice enters.

Maurice I finally got him to rest, my father.

Rachel Did he know who you were?

Maurice He thought I was you at first. When I told him you were in the garden, he then started calling me Charlie. He's started to confuse us, one for the other. I'm Maurice, Dad, I said, Maurice, the youngest. He repeated my name and asked me what I wanted. I said, try to get a bit of sleep. I had just put my hand into my Da's hand and I'd put him to bed. I took off his shoes and socks –

Charlie Did he let you kiss him?

Maurice I didn't try.

Rachel You didn't dare.

Maurice No, I didn't.

Charlie You'll have to teach us –

Maurice To take care of him? I'm willing to stay. I'm willing to learn, if that is what's going to happen. Is it?

Rachel Who can say?

Jane He can say.

Rachel My father?

Jane Let him have his say.

Charlie When?

Jane Wait for him to waken.

Maurice And then?

Jane Let him decide. As always. Let him make up his mind what he wants to happen.

Charlie What's left of his mind.

Jane There's enough.

Charlie Little enough.

Jane His little enough is more than most people's plenty.

Charlie Ma, if he's had a chance to sleep, maybe you should let him.

Jane Give him more consideration than he's ever given me.

Charlie Who drummed that into us? You did, Mother. We learned not to bother him. Not to bother you. Work to be done. Important work.

Jane And it was done.

Charlie At all costs.

Rachel No matter who was neglected.

Jane Nobody was neglected. Stop that sob story. What is worse than adults whining about their parents? Will you at last turn into adult men and women?

Rachel As my father turns back to being a child.

Maurice I think we should let him sleep.

Jane Do you all think so? Three against one. So be it. We'll face this when he wakens. Now, I have work to do.

Maurice Why don't you just sit down? For once sit down, talk to us.

Jane I'm not sure I want to – if it's not my humour?

Maurice Why not?

Jane What if there's nothing to say, unless he's here?

Maurice You've barely spoken to me since I've come home.

Jane Nor you to me, but at least you still call here home.

Maurice Should I not?

Jane touches Maurice's cheek and embraces him tightly, then pulls his hair gently.

Jane Does that answer you?

Maurice What should we do, Mother?

Jane What he says – your father.

Rachel And you'll do that?

Jane Don't I always? Is that not what I am? The obedient wife. Do you agree?

Silence.

Maybe not. How do I convince you? How would he? Tell you a story? Here's one to tickle your fancy. There was once a couple – a very ancient couple who used to beat the lining out of each other. One day they kicked each other into their solicitor's office. He asked them why they were here? We want a divorce. A divorce – why? We hate each other. How long are you married? Seventy years. How long do you hate each other? Seventy years. We want a divorce. But why wait seventy years to divorce? We had to wait till the children were dead.

She looks at them one by one.

Well, children, you are not dead. And you've not divorced us. Thank you. Fetch him.

Jane goes back to working in the garden.

You two, I could do with a hand here. Fetch your father.

Maurice exits.
Rachel and Charlie help Jane in the garden, and she lets them.

SCENE FIVE

The light is now turning into late evening, and Jane, Charlie and Rachel sit in the garden.
Maurice enters, hand in hand with Sam.
Sam wears a pyjama jacket and the trousers he has been wearing throughout the play.
His feet are bare.

Sam I have no socks on.

Jane Do you want your shoes and socks?

Sam No – I was just saying I did not wearing them.

Jane 'Did not wearing' – what are you talking about?

Sam Socks.

Maurice Where do you keep your socks?

Sam In my shoes.

Maurice That makes sense.

Sam Why should it not?

Jane Why not indeed? Maurice, go and get them.

Maurice exits.

So, Sam, how have you spent your day?

Sam Doing nothing.

Jane Absolutely nothing? Just sitting spinning yarns –

Sam Yarns?

Jane About me. All my misdemeanours. Such gruesome scenarios. From what pit do they enter your head? I don't want to know. Maybe I should though. Maybe they're all that is to be known about you. Hearing them, do I see you for what you are?

Sam Which is what?

Jane A man who leads his life at one remove from all he is, sitting there watching himself, asking – what if there is nothing to watch? What if there never has been? Nothing inside nor outside, nothing whatsoever. Your family – your writing – your life, worth nothing? How do you deal with that? You go mad, my dear. You are going mad. And you will not be content until you drive us that way, or you drive us all apart.

Maurice returns with the slippers and socks.

Sam I am sorry.

Maurice hands the slippers and socks to Sam.

I am very sorry.

Sam looks at Rachel.

Yes, I am sorry. You see, I am not wearing socks.

Maurice You have them in your arms.

Sam That is not the point. The point is I have forgotten how to put them on. I know what to do with shoes. I know where they go. And I know there is some connection between shoes and socks, but for the life of me, I cannot remember what. Will you help me?

Maurice kneels and puts Sam's slipper and sock on his right foot.

Sam Thank you.

Maurice puts Sam's other slipper and sock on his left foot.

Now I am dressed.

Charlie Why didn't you say sorry to me? You said sorry to Maurice and to Rachel. Not to me nor to mother, why?

Sam You didn't deserve it.

Charlie Why not?

Sam You both did well out of me. Remarkably well.

Charlie As you did out of us.

Sam Then thank you. The two of you, thanks. And in return, what do you say back to me?

Charlie What should we say?

Sam A thank you in return would suffice.

Charlie No, Father, that would choke me.

Sam And you, Jane, are you in choking mood? The slow joys of strangulation, happy to squeeze the air out of the argument, turn blue with pleasure, just let rip and say, thanks.

Jane No.

Sam Why not?

Jane Because it would divert from the task in hand. You're the great master of diversion, Sam. Not going to work this time. We're going to tell you what we're thinking –

Charlie We were thinking how we're going to manage you if your mind gets any more confused. We were thinking how soon before you needed proper nursing – professional nursing – either here or in a home. We were wondering if you would agree to it, or would you have to be forced. Sorry to be so blunt telling you.

Sam You are tired of me, Charlie.

Charlie Very tired. Exhausted.

Sam And you, Jane – also exhausted?

Silence.

The cat has got your tongues. What a wonderful thought. Exquisite things, cats' tongues. All sharp and pink, lapping white milk, their music the sound of their tasting, slowly, lovingly, draining the dish dry. May I have some?

Rachel What?

Sam Milk.

Jane Why?

Sam I am thirsty.

Rachel Then get him milk.

Sam Don't. I changed my mind. The prerogative of the lunatic. No? Well, isn't that what you think I am?

Maurice Me and Rachel, we didn't say that.

Sam But you think it, and you should, for it's right. And I must deal with it. There is no remedy for what afflicts

67

me, wear and tear, age and fear – fear of life, fear of death. So what is to become of me in this affliction? Can any of you give me an answer?

Silence.

My wife told me to die. Last night I was dreaming – no, it was today – I was dying – Or was I driving, driving again, from Donegal to Dublin, down that endless road, cutting through Derry, and then for the life of me I could not remember where next. But the car kept driving, taking me where – where would I be travelling?

Charlie Strabane and Omagh –

Maurice Aughnacloy and Emyvale –

Rachel Monaghan, Ardee –

Charlie And straight into Dublin –

Sam All the way there I could hear someone weeping, in the back of the car, saying I have youngsters – children – are you going to kill me? I was sure it was a woman, but when I looked behind, no one was there. Then it hit me as we drove on to the coast. That's where she was leading me, the woman crying. Was she me, wanting to die, walk into the Irish Sea, ask the sea to kill me, let the cold kill me? Will you let me do that? Will you help me to die? Jane?

Jane Never.

Sam Children, help me to die.

Rachel Never.

Maurice Never.

Charlie None of us will do that. Never look to us for help there.

Sam Never? Right – the end of story. There was once a man spent his life writing stories. Now, as he reads them, he cannot remember a single word. Who was it wrote that? No one. What is he reading? Nothing. As I say, end of story, if you let me end it. Let me die, will you?

Silence.

Who will hear this heathen calling for hope?

He beats the ground with his slippered feet.

Great Satan, let me enter the kingdom of darkness and fire – let me in, let me die. Let me paddle in your pools of shit and drink the piss of the damned. Great Baal and his priests, give me a sign. Will you accept me as human sacrifice?

Silence.

Will you let me spill my blood and bones? Here in this garden? How high is the highest tree?

Jane High enough.

Sam What if I climb it? Fall –

Jane And break your neck? There's a simpler way of going, Sam, an easier way.

Sam Which is?

Jane Waiting.

Sam Waiting for the end? Will I be allowed to do so? Will you allow me? What do you say to that, Jane?

Jane I say I will stand by you.

Sam As I wait?

Jane You've heard what I said.

Sam You will wait with me?

Jane Waiting in the sands?

Sam Waiting to be let go? Waiting to be found?

Jane If that is what you wish.

Sam It is.

Jane Then so be it.

Sam Yes. So be it.

Jane Yes.

Charlie Do you know what they're saying to each other?

Maurice I only hear what you hear.

Rachel Our father is going to live, live here, with mother minding him.

Charlie And me – just in case you're forgetting, me –

Maurice And us –

Rachel The two of us as well. We will stay –

Charlie Till they write the next cheque. Then you're gone –

Rachel Not this time.

Charlie Every time, Rachel. Stay here with the two of them? You wouldn't last a month. You can barely stick them when they're well – what will you be like when they're sick?

Rachel You deserve to be who you are.

Charlie Keep off the streets, Rachel.

Rachel Scraped off the streets, would that be more to your liking, Charlie? The only kind of woman you know – the only kind of woman you'll get.

Charlie That will be paid back.

Jane And what have you been doing, Maurice?

Silence.

Sam My silent son, will you tell us?

Maurice Recovering.

Jane What from?

Maurice Heart.

Jane Broken?

Maurice Broken, broke, breaking –

Sam Breaking.

Silence.

Charlie It was another man, wasn't it?

Maurice If you say so.

Charlie Well done, Maurice – bringing more credit to the house.

Maurice What do you expect in Babylon?

Jane Who was the man?

Maurice A man who let me face up to myself. He made me stop telling lies. Lies that I've lived a long time. With him I began to tell myself the truth. For that I thanked him. Thanks was not enough. He left. I don't know why. Maybe he just wearied of me not being able to say what he wanted to hear. I could not tell him that I needed him. I loved him. The sun, the moon, the stars in the sky – they've all gone out. I can't see where I will go. That's why I've come home. To ask for help.

Silence.

Rachel I'll need help as well, Maurice. I'll want a hand with the baby. I'd be grateful for your support. If you like, we can stick together.

Maurice Do you mean here? All right. It will be a wonderful child.

Jane It will be a child. I'd better ask when it's due.

Jane gently touches Rachel's belly.

Five, six months, you'll deliver, am I right?

Rachel That's when I will blossom, mother. Have your shears ready.

Jane and Rachel laugh together.

Sam Who was the man who left you, Maurice? Was he older than you?

Maurice Yes.

Sam Was he ashamed to meet us? Were you ashamed of him? I'd like to think you will all feel free to do just that – bring shame on this house. That would be my wish.

Charlie And it's been well granted. You call me a stupid donkey, but look at what else you've reared – the happy family bailing each other out. You have them now to tend you all your days – the whore and the queer.

Rachel Donkey, Charlie? Wrong choice of creature. Dirty big dinosaur more like.

Charlie At least I stood on my own two feet –

Rachel You have never in your life stood on their own two feet.

Charlie Have you?

Maurice We tried.

Charlie Why was I not let do the same?

He turns to Jane and Sam.

Was it because I would have failed? Have I failed the two of you?

Jane You think you have – you're wrong in that. You succeeded in staying. In this house that was not easy, but you did it, and I'm grateful.

Charlie Then you want me to stay with you?

Jane Yes.

Charlie You need me?

Jane We do. We all do, son.

Charlie Thank you.

Silence.

And I will try to love the baby. I say, I will try to.

Rachel goes to embrace Charlie, who shrugs her away.

What do you think you're at?

Jane Charlie's getting cross again. It must be getting near time for bed.

Rachel Not that late.

Jane That girl would sit up till it was morning.

Rachel The sunrise over Lough Swilly – the White Strand in a blaze of red light –

Maurice Spectacular.

Sam The birds going mad –

Jane Will I make a picnic and we'll sit up – eating and drinking and waiting for the sun?

Charlie I'm hitting the hay. Da, you need your rest. I warn you I'm not missing my kip. I'm like a bear if I don't get a good night's sleep.

Maurice None of us are exactly pleasant in the morning.

Rachel Who would want to be?

Jane My mother. She loved the early hours of daylight. You didn't know her when she was a young woman. She'd turned into an old bitch by the time you'd met her, wanting nobody near her, hating the world. There was a time though – she was full of singing, full of songs. They were how her mother learned words of English. Some so lovely, so arcane.

Sam Arcane. I remember. I do recall that. This makes sense to me, what you're saying. And so do you, Charlie. You're being wise. We should be going to bed, the lot of us.

Jane Tell them a story, Sam. If you're making sense, tell them another story, the children. A new one nobody's ever heard before.

Sam The kind I make up as I go along?

Jane The best kind.

Sam Where do I start?

Jane Once upon a time –

Sam There was a man who had three fields.

Rachel Were they large fields?

Sam Very large. He owned the fields and he owned a forest.

Maurice What grew in the forest?

Charlie Trees.

Maurice What kind of trees?

Sam Trees as red as blood, trees warm as fire – the trees of this garden. The man decided to build a big house.

74

Charlie A mansion?

Maurice A fortress?

Rachel A palace?

Sam A big house that would be a mansion and a fortress and a palace, in the three fields beside his forest.

Charlie Were there animals in the forest?

Rachel Antelopes and gazelles?

Maurice Bears and giants?

Charlie Was there a witch in the forest?

Sam You could call her a witch – she called herself something else.

Maurice What?

Sam I'm going to let you guess that.

Charlie Why don't you let me guess? It was me asked was there a witch –

Sam She put a spell on the trees of the forest and the man could not cut them down to construct his great house –

Charlie Why didn't he use cement?

Sam Why don't you listen to the story?

Charlie Well, why didn't he?

Sam The trees of the forest refused him their timber. So he was left with the dilemma – out of what can I build my mansion, my fortress, my palace? The birds of the air heard him ask that question. They saw his distress, so they sang to him. He thought he could hear words in their music, and guess what the words were? Make your refuge out of what is most dear to you. That way it will

75

stand against all your enemies. It will last forever. Just
then the man saw his children playing in the fields beside
the forest. Out of their flesh he fashioned his house –
their blood and bones, their hands and hearts, their
minds and heads, their knees and toes, their tongues,
their nails. He did not stop – never stopping till the work
was done. Then he stood in the empty mansion, the
lonely fortress, the haunted palace. He heard silence –
eternal silence, the silence of the spheres whose music
had stopped, the spheres rotating in space, the gigantic,
galactic space between his ears, the stupid, stupid man
who sacrificed his children. He knew what he had done,
and it scared the life out of him. He ran outside and he
shouted at the sky. Give me back my little ones. But the
sky laughed in his face, and there was no one else to tell,
no one but the trees of the forest and the woman who
lived there. He ran to it, to her, and he asked this. What
should I do to stop the silence? She told him. Shake the
trees that grow in your garden, the trees you could not
cut down. Shake them. See what happens. The man did
so. From their red branches his children fell, straight into
his arms, alive and kicking into the garden, where they
went on playing.

Charlie What happened to the big house?

Maurice The fortress?

Rachel The palace?

Sam Ask your mother.

Jane His wife sold it for a fortune to a developer. He
wanted to turn it into luxury apartments. Then the
property boom went bust and the developer, who was a
complete chancer, was left on his uppers. So he was only
too delighted to sell it back to her for a fraction of what
he'd paid for it. That was how they all lived happily, if

not quite ever after, then for as long as the windfall lasted. From this, learn a lesson. It may be the way your father tells them, but your mother knows the value of a pound.

Maurice Thanks for the story, Da.

Charlie I didn't understand it. Was I meant to? No, likely not. And I suppose I should not have said that either. You could take me nowhere. I'm remarking on that before the rest of you can get a chance.

Rachel You look very far away, Daddy. What are you thinking about? What are you hearing?

Sam The birds. When it all goes, I'll miss their voices, recognising them.

Rachel The moon's rising.

Jane sings, the Children joining in.

Jane/Children
I watched last night the rising moon
     Upon a foreign strand,
Till memories came like flowers in June
     Of home and fatherland.
I dreamt I was a child once more
     Beside the rippling rill,
When first I saw in days of yore
     The moon behind the hill.

It brought me back the visions grand
     That purpled boyhood's dreams,
Its youthful loves, its happy land
     As bright as morning beams.
It brought me back the spreading lea,
     The steeple and the mill,
Until my eyes could scarcely see
     The moon behind the hill.

And there beneath the silv'ry sky
    I lived life once again,
I counted all the hopes gone by,
    I wept at all the pain.
    And when I'm gone, oh may some tongue
The minstrel's wish fulfil
    And still remember me who sang
    The moon behind the hill.

Jane sings alone.

Jane
    And still remember me who sang
    The moon behind the hill.

Silence.

She sang that, my mother. She taught me, just listening
to her. I must have taught you. And I remember clearly
when I sang that and couldn't stop – just after she died –
it was all I could hear.

Sam What was it?

Maurice What was what?

Sam The song. Was it called 'Danny Boy'?

Jane How would it be 'Danny Boy'? It's 'The Moon
Behind the Hill'.

Sam Do I know that?

Jane You must, Sam – my mother's song. I thought I
would never get over her. I thought my heart would
break when she died – and it was all I could hear, her
singing that song.

Sam Did I know the words? The words – the words –

Charlie To what, Da?

Sam To what you were singing – what you were – were –

Sam starts to get angry.

What you were singing. What were you singing? The words – the words –

Jane Sam, what's wrong with you?

Sam shouts.

Sam The words – the words – I forget –

Jane starts to shake Sam.

Jane Enough –

Sam Words –

Jane Sam, look me in the face –

Sam Who are you?

Rachel Let him go, Ma.

Sam Who are you?

Rachel Let him go.

Jane lets Sam go, but he is still in distress.

Sam What is the word?

Charlie It's all starting.

Maurice Beginning of the end.

Sam I forgot the word.

Jane For song?

Sam Song, yes.

Rachel Father.

Sam That's it.

Maurice Father.

Sam The words.

Charlie Father.

Sam I forgot the song for word.

A bird sings somewhere in the distance.

The song for – word – word – word –

He attempts to say 'word'.

Word –

Night has now fallen, turning the family into shadows.
    Rain starts to fall.
    The strange music recurs.
    He again attempts to say 'word'.

Word.